LIGHTNING BOLT BOOKS™

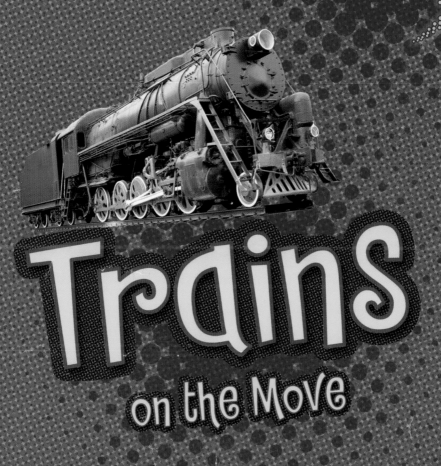

Trains
on the Move

Lee Sullivan Hill

Lerner Publications Company
Minneapolis

To my sister
Amy –L.S.H.

Lerner Publications Company
A division of Lerner Publishing Group, Inc.
241 First Avenue North
Minneapolis, MN 55401 U.S.A.

Website address: www.lernerbooks.com

Library of Congress Cataloging-in-Publication Data

Hill, Lee Sullivan, 1958–
    Trains on the move / by Lee Sullivan Hill.
        p.   cm. — (Lightning bolt books ™ — vroom-vroom)
    Includes index.
    ISBN 978–0–7613–3921–2 (lib. bdg. : alk. paper)
    1. Railroad trains—Juvenile literature. I. Title.
    TF148.H55 2011
    625.1—dc22   2010018170

Manufactured in the United States of America
1 — CG — 12/31/10

Contents

Train Parts

RUMBLE! ROAR!

Here comes a train.
What do you see first?

Locomotives lead the way. They pull the train along a track.

A bright orange locomotive chugs down a railroad track.

Train cars follow.
CLICKETY-CLACK!

Can you count the cars?

This train has three locomotives and too many cars to count. The cars carry goods like apples and toys. Goods on a train are called freight.

What Trains Carry

Some freight rides inside boxcars. Big doors slide open for loading.

Hopper cars are loaded from the top. These hoppers carry coal.

Tanker cars hold liquids like corn syrup. Tankers look like cans on wheels.

Flatcars are flat. Freight rides on the top. Some flatcars carry freight in containers. Freight containers look like giant boxes.

These are freight containers.

What kind of freight does this train carry?

**None!
It carries
people.**

Trains and People

People who ride trains are called passengers. They get on and off trains at a railroad station.

Passengers eat in dining cars.

They sleep in sleeper cars.

This boy rests in a sleeper car bed.

Coach cars have rows of seats.

Bi-level cars have an upstairs and a downstairs.

Can you count the windows?

Train Control

Trains need people to make them go. Engineers run the trains. Engineers ride high up in a cab.

Signals help engineers. These lights tell which track to follow and how fast to go.

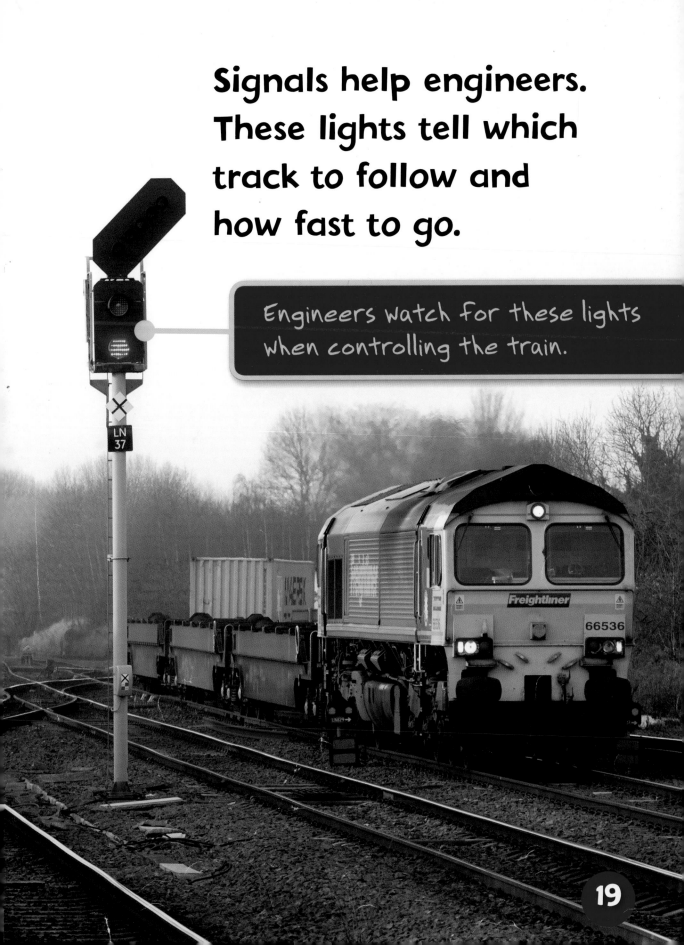

Engineers watch for these lights when controlling the train.

The engineer does not need to steer. Train wheels fit tightly on the track. The train goes where the track goes.

Trains change tracks to change direction. Switches help trains move from track to track.

Many switches and tracks are in a train yard. The yard is where trains are put together. Yard locomotives push cars in place.

The cars bump end to end.
BAM! Couplers lock the
cars together.

FRED goes on the end of a train. FRED is not a person. It is a Flashing Rear End Device. It tells the engineer if another train is close.

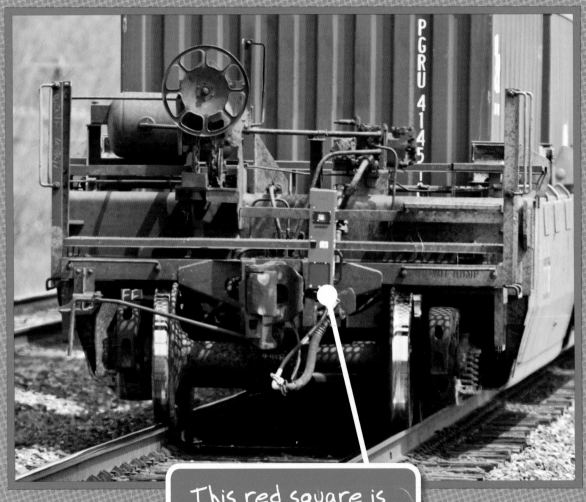

This red square is the Flashing Rear End Device.

Train Tasks

This train is on its way. It will haul freight across the country.

8363

This train takes passengers to work in a city.

Trains carry goods. They carry people. Are you ready to hop on board?

The conductor makes sure everyone is on the train before pulling out of the station.

Train Car Diagrams

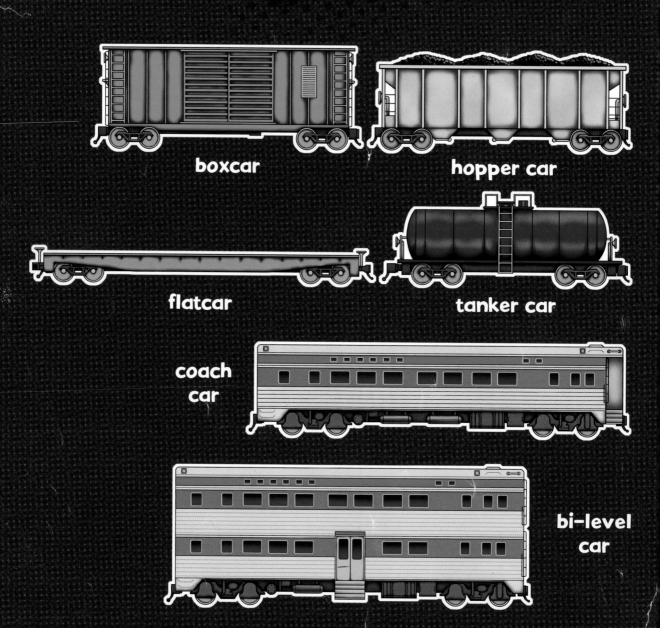

boxcar

hopper car

flatcar

tanker car

coach car

bi-level car

Fun Facts

- Railroads have been running in the United States for more than 175 years. The first trains were pulled by horses.

- You can ride an Amtrak passenger train in forty-five of the fifty states. Many passenger trains carry mail as well as people.

- The Burlington Northern Santa Fe Railway ships enough sugar each year to make more than three billion batches of cookies!

- Trucks can ride on trains too. When a truck trailer rides on a flatcar, it's called piggybacking.

- The longest train in the entire world ran in South Africa in 1989. It had 660 cars and stretched more than 4 miles (6 kilometers)!

Glossary

coupler: a metal piece that joins train cars together

engineer: a person who runs a train

FRED: a Flashing Rear End Device. It goes on the end of a train and tells the engineer when another train is near.

freight: goods that are carried on a train

locomotive: the machine that pulls a train

passenger: a person who rides a train

signal: a light that tells a train where to go and how fast

switch: a control that helps a train change tracks

Further Reading

Enchanted Learning: Vehicle Online Coloring Pages
http://www.enchantedlearning.com/vehicles/
paintonline.shtml

Hubbell, Patricia. *Trains: Steaming! Pulling! Huffing!* Tarrytown, NY: Marshall Cavendish, 2005.

Krensky, Stephen. *Casey Jones.* Minneapolis: Millbrook Press, 2007.

Transit People: The Train Era
http://www.transitpeople.org/lesson/train.htm

Von Finn, Denny. *Bullet Trains.* Minneapolis: Bellwether Media, 2010.

Index

Photo Acknowledgments

The images in this book are used with the permission of: ©Alexander Kalina/Shutterstock Images, p. 1; © iStockphoto.com/Kenneth Sponsler, p. 2; © Peter Titmuss/Alamy, pp. 4, 13, 17; © Steve Crise/Transtock Inc./Alamy, p. 5; © John Elk III/Alamy, p. 6; © David R. Frazier Photolibrary, Inc./Alamy, p. 7; © Howard Ande, p. 8; © Jim Parkin/Alamy, pp. 9, 26; © Fotog/Tetra Images/Photolibrary, p. 10; © Tom Kraft/Transtock, Inc./Alamy, p. 11, 24; © Ted Foxx/Alamy, p. 12; © Jim West/Alamy, pp. 14, 27; © Nick North/Surf/CORBIS, p. 15; © Paul Springett 08/Alamy, p. 16; © Rufus Stone/Alamy, p. 18; © Colin Underhill/Alamy, p. 19; © Dean Fox/SuperStock, p. 20; © Dirk Enters/Imagebroker/Alamy, p. 21; © Keith Douglas/Alamy, p. 22; © Trains and Planes/Alamy, p. 23; © Ambient Images, Inc./SuperStock, p. 25; © Laura Westlund/Independent Picture Service, p. 28; © Ana de Sousa/Shutterstock Images, p. 30; © iStockphoto.com/Rick Sargeant, p. 31.

Front cover: © iStockphoto.com/ Kjell Stén, (Black Locomotive, side); © Belinda Images/SuperStock, (Red Locomotive, front).